Results Matter

How smart people hire smart real estate agents

Nancy G Gardner

ISBN: 1492104221
ISBN 13: 9781492104223
Library of Congress Control Number: 2013914892
CreateSpace Independent Publishing Platform
North Charleston, South Carolina

Posthumous Dedication

Mary Louise Waggoner Grimes

my Mother

TABLE OF CONTENTS

PREFACE

I've heard this story a lot – I'll bet you have too

I was deplaning recently and struck up a conversation with a passenger who, after learning that I was a real estate consultant/trainer told me that she was trying to sell her mother's home in NJ. She said that the house had been on the market for over a year – initially listed @ $230,000 and now reduced to @ $139,000. She mentioned that she had rejected an offer early on and wished that she had taken it. I asked her what her agent advised and she said that the agent had counseled her not to take the offer– even though research shows that the first offer is usually the best – and it was her agent's job to know this information.

This got me thinking about how many times I'd had similar conversations – friends and acquaintances relaying stories of properties that were not priced correctly; long drawn out times on the market which resulted in even lower eventual sales prices; the high cost of carrying the property until it sold and the inconvenience of it all with little or no communication from their agent during the process. To add insult to injury, they paid commissions totaling thousands of dollars to people who had cost them money.

I have trained management and agents in the real estate industry for more than a dozen years and I have experienced this lack of skill first hand. I am amazed how little training and even less accountability there is in the industry. There is a lot of talk about 'service and caring' but a deficit in functional and operational knowledge to back these claims. A positive result for the client speaks volumes in terms of service and caring. I wrote this book to that end – to help real estate buyers and sellers weed through the plethora of agents and figure out how to pick the right one for their home sale or purchase.

Now you as a consumer will have access to the information you need in order to choose a qualified real estate agent and get your money's worth! Once you find an agent with the required skill level – it is then your job to listen to them and take their professional advice – much the same way you would for any other skilled professional you'd hire. This book is divided into two sections. The first section addresses 'Sellers' information and the second is written to guide the 'Buyer' though the real estate transaction.

INTRODUCTION

Let's Get Started with a Brief History of Recent Events

Real estate is the largest single purchase most people make in their lifetimes. How is it, then, that many of the people we hire to handle this important transaction have had little or no training and the companies they work for have little or no idea what their agents are doing out in the marketplace?

Real estate has been primarily a relationship business. With all the new ways we are able to connect online – it's even easier to maintain those relationships today.

In recent years, there have been significant changes that have had an important impact on those relationships. One consequence of the economic crash, the bailouts, the stimulus, loss

of middle class jobs, short sales and foreclosures is that an angry and mistrustful consumer
has emerged. Consumers trust neither govern-
ment nor business – and often for good reason.

The media reports that "real estate is back' –
there is an underlying story here that isn't
getting much press. In many markets, the
resurgence in home buying is due mainly to
investors. Hedge funds are buying up a lot of
real estate and most are cash buyers. Continued
pressure on middle class jobs and damaged
credit along with tight lending standards still
make it difficult for many to buy.

For those who are able to buy a home, the
stakes have changed – houses are no longer
ATM's – and it's more important than ever
to hire someone who can get the job done in
today's challenging market conditions. How
does the consumer know that the agent that
they are hiring and paying thousands of dollars (5-6% of the sales price in most markets
– though negotiable) has the requisite skills?

According to study done by the WAV Group
- a real estate consulting and research group –
"January – June 2014,

39% of real estate licensees had no listings

50% of real estate licensees had 1- 10 listings

7% or real estate licensees had 11-20 listings

3% of real estate licensees had 21 – 50 listings

1% of real estate licensees had 51+ listings"

The next relevant question might be, "What percentage of the listings taken actually sold?"

Today, the consumer wants and deserves competence and transparency – easier to write about than to find when we go looking for it. Does the designation of "Top Producer" and "Market Share Leader" assure us of results – maybe – maybe not?

You gotta have trust. And that's the main reason we seek out someone we know or who is recommended to us. If your standard of trust is that you 'get along' or they tell you what you want to hear – then none of the rest of this matters. If hiring a professional who gives you competent advice and guidance – and has the performance results to back up their claims – I believe the trust you seek will be there. The rest of the selection process will be subjective based on *your preferences.*

In this book, you will learn an objective approach to:

What you should be able to expect from your agent,

What questions to ask to determine their ability to get results for their clients and

Areas in the transaction where conflicts of interest may arise

The rest of the selection process is subjective and preferences differ among individuals.

I have trained management and agents in the real estate industry since 1997. There are companies and agents who do the work and are a credit to the industry. Many are not receptive to doing the work required to insure that you, the consumer, come first in the transaction. Some are betting on technology and social media solving their issues. Some believe that a discounted online approach will be the answer.

Real customer service exists ONLY when the agent involved works at a level that guarantees that you receive the skill required to navigate challenging market and liquidity conditions and provides the measured data to back up their claims. Look for reviews and performance data that demonstrate consistency in both.

Again, once you find such a professional, it is your job as a motivated buyer or seller, to listen to the advice and counsel that these professionals provide. It's tough to get well when you don't listen to your doctor.

SELLER'S GUIDE TO HIRING

AN AGENT

PART ONE

The Smart Seller's Guide to Hiring a Qualified Real Estate Agent

Your Motivation Matters

You have made the decision to sell your house. Motivation is critical. In today's post recession world, consider the uneven recovery and the changes in the consumer – skeptical, angry and mistrustful.

There are always markets that enjoy a faster rebound when conditions improve. Competitive pricing still brings buyers in the door. In most real estate markets, "bubble pricing" (home prices at the top of the market) is not the norm – and interestingly, even in strong markets, attracting the buyer through proper pricing is important – even though the buyer may end up in a bidding war escalating your price. In the buyer's mind the difference is that they chose to increase their offer. In these same strong markets, properties will sit unsold because they are priced too high to attract today's buyer – hence the term 'stale listings'.

Approach this process only when you are serious about getting your home sold. In today's market, longer time on the market means less money to you – most markets are showing improvement and the distressed inventory is also in decline. Add to these hopeful signs, a slow improvement in unemployment and under employment and tight financing and appraisal conditions – be serious about getting your home sold before going forward. It will pay you to understand that the recovery is uneven. Let the market stats and pricing research for your locale guide you.

Getting Your House Ready to Market

Most of what needs to happen as you begin this process to sell must happen to your mindset – your house may not be worth as much as it once was – and in most cases money has been taken out of the property along the way to pay for other things via home equity loans. The value of your property can vary based on the economic fundamentals where you live, the location and condition of your property etc. Coming to grips with this is important and is reflected in pricing your home to sell and the eventual time it sits on the market. Time is money – and it's out of your pocket.

Making Improvements – when and what?

Before you make any improvements – let your real estate agent guide you. It's part of the full service that you are paying for – and can save you money. A professional agent will guide you on what needs to be done and what won't matter to the consumer – so hold off until you get guidance from the professional you hire to sell your home. It helps to understand that the way you live in your home and the way that you sell your home are two different things.

Professional agents may have your home '**staged**' so that it will show in the best possible light to potential buyers. Some agents have been trained in staging and they can advise you. Again, it is a part of a full-service commission.

START YOUR SEARCH ENGINES PLEASE – FINDING A QUALIFIED PROFESSIONAL

Referral

Most people choose someone through *referral* – an agent you know or have used before – so you can start there – just be prepared that it might not end there. Friendship is not a necessary requirement – the point is to hire someone who serves your interests and can get the job done. Let **objective** criteria guide you first.

Check out agents/companies online. Make sure the company/agent has a visible presence on the web. Over 90% of buyers looked online first –so make sure you like what you see. Look for testimonials with specifics and pay attention to what they say.

Most companies are represented on multiple sites: Realtor.com; Trulia; Zillow and more. In addition, look at how their listing inventory is presented. Does the company's listing inventory **consistently** have videos/ slide shows and complete information? Is their website mobile?

All listings should have current tours/videos – if some listings are absent these – this could happen to you as well. Listings without slide shows/ videos are ignored on the web. The agent didn't bother – why should the consumer?

Interview 2-3 agents. (Details of the interview expectations will follow.) Make appointments for separate days if possible. Do not get pressured in to making the listing decision until you have finished interviewing – you are paying a lot for these services – make the effort.

Second to using objective criteria will be your 'comfort level' with the agent. This is hard to measure and varies with the individual and it is also a factor. Once you have obtained objective measures, then the comfort level is left for you to determine based on your own criteria.

Top Producers
You might assume that hiring only top agents is the way to go. "It ain't necessarily so". Focus on actual results at whatever level an agent produces. Volume is not a sure sign of service and while results an agent obtains for their clients is paramount – there are other considerations that may be important to you as well. **The selection of an agent is both objective and subjective.**

One of the top ten agents in a market forgot to provide the Homeowner's Association Documents to the buyer within the time prescribed by the state law. At the settlement, the buyer walked away from the purchase and the seller had no recourse. Busy agents don't always cross their 't's'.

ASK: *Given the amount of business you do, what systems do you have in place that will ensure that things don't fall through the cracks? How often can I expect communication from you? What written service guarantees do you offer?*

Agent Teams

Are you better off hiring a 'team' to represent you in the sale of your home? The same objective criteria apply to their results. Another useful measure is to ask about the per person production for the team members. A lot of teams are run no better than traditional brokerages. Just ask the questions that will give you the confidence in hiring the right professional for you.

New Agents

Should you hire an agent that lacks experience? Some new agents are better trained than their more experienced counterparts. Look for company/office averages for the results they have obtained for their clients. Ask for information about the company training program they have completed and also what managerial oversight will be given during the transaction.

Online Agent Rankings

Objective information about agents is beginning to show up online. Trulia and Zillow are posting agent reviews and recently Realtor.com requested 'SOLDS' data on agents. To be fair, MLS' operate differently and oft times skew the data you need. There are efforts to standardize data reporting across all MLS'. Most online agent reviews are subjective – and while helpful, it's better to begin with objective information concerning an agent's results. When online reviews turn into online rankings based on an agent's results, they'll be much more useful to you. Imagine being able to pull agent data the way we pull flight data and pricing on online sites.

If you're checking an agent out on **social media** sites – recommendations will vary – and you may have a tough time figuring out the source – which could be a fellow agent, their broker or their grandmother. In short, it's hard to get the objective info you need in order to make your hiring decision with confidence.

Some real estate professionals have gotten out in front of the issues of results and transparency. These agents have put a link in their email signature that gives an accounting of their results. Some have added this data into their agent profiles and onto their websites/pages. Careful here, some misrepresent themselves – verify when you can by checking the history of listed properties.

A client of mine told me of a recent listing appointment where the seller asked for an accounting of his professional results – which were accurately provided – the seller hired them on the spot. The Seller went on to tell them of an agent he'd interviewed the previous day that had misrepresented his Days On Market stat giving the seller days on market since the last price reduction rather than counted from the original listing period. Because the seller had done some research beforehand, he knew the agent was lying and threw him out.

Agent review sites
You may locate helpful real estate agent profiles and reviews on the following:
    Zillow.com
    Trulia.com
    Redfin.com (not in all markets)
    Realtor.com (coming soon)
    Yahoo.com
    Yelp.com
    Google+Local
    Facebook

Realsatisfied.com
Stik.com
Zufog.com
Reach150.com
RealEstateRatingz.com
HomeThinking.com
IncredibleAgents.com
RateMyAgent.com
NeighborCity.com
TopAgentsRanked.com
Angie's List
Yahoo Local
Citysearch
Insider Pages
LinkedIn
Har.com (Houston TX market)

Early in 2105, Zillow's acquisition of Trulia was finalized. However, the new company is organized, this should mean better technology and more information.

In 2014, News Corp. acquired Move, Inc. – meaning Realtor.com – again this should mean more and better information for you, the consumers. At this writing (2105) Realtor. com has requested SOLD data on agents from the MLS.

Fingers crossed.

INTERVIEW AND HIRE LIKE A PRO

Before the listing appointment
Expect a call from a potential listing agent (or their assistant) setting the time to meet and to answer a few pre-appointment questions so that the agent can prepare for the appointment. Most agents will make two appointments.

The first appointment is to view your property for condition and amenities and in some cases, the agent can/will recommend service vendors who can make any needed repairs, etc. should you need them.

The second appointment is for the actual Listing Presentation and Proposal. I recommend that this be conducted at the agent's office – doing so will take you away from any emotion you may feel in moving – and you'll be clearer to make your decision.

The Listing Presentation
The professional agent will give you a presentation containing the following:

Current market conditions (specific to your area) and how these conditions will affect your ability to sell. Market statistics will give you a clear idea of the competition you'll face in selling as well as other issues that you may encounter.

Current financial climate – an accounting of lending and appraisal issues and interest rates in your market and how they can affect a buyer's ability to buy and close the purchase.

Agent's performance results – these stats showcase their ability to get results for their clients under **current** market conditions.

Representation – your options *vary by state* as to how you can be represented in the sale of your home.

A marketing proposal – how their approach differentiates from the competition and benefits you.

A pricing proposal – you should expect the absorption rate pricing analysis (I'll explain below) to be used to adequately reflect your competition in the sale of your property.

An overview of the administrative process – disclosures, agreements etc. and the process that ensues.

Presentation Detail
Do not confuse data with knowledge. Expect an agent who understands current market conditions and how they affect your ability to sell your property and who can communicate the information clearly.

Market Data that you'll want to have a basic understanding of are:

Listing Inventory: year over year and percentage of difference; the higher the inventory the more competition you have – and more pressure on pricing. You need to have a clear picture of current inventory – it's your competition – and how this number will affect your ability to sell.

Pending Sales: year over year and percentage of difference; – in some markets there is a lot of 'fall-thru' (contracts ratified but do not close) - have agent discuss reasons. Also, ask agent for their percentage of fall-through – a properly trained agent can prevent much of this.

Closed Sales: year over year and percentage of difference – financing challenges persist.

Days on Market: the average amount of time properties are on the market before going 'under contract'.

Average Sales Price: year over year and percentage of change; and may be a good indicator how much pricing has declined (or risen) in the last twelve months – add to that the overall decrease since the peak of the housing bubble (2006). Even in markets that have low listing inventories – most pricing has not returned to pre-crisis levels. As of this writing (summer of 2014) there are only 5-6 markets that have regained the pricing lost in the recession.

% Of Distressed Sales in your market: Buyers are being taught (mostly by the media) that these offer the best pricing, etc., which is not always true, and another reason that the agent you hire has to have a strong pricing record. The numbers may **vary widely by state**. This is further complicated by second mortgages coming due. About half of these second mortgages were issued between 2004 – 2006, when prices were in a different place. These second mortgages coming due will likely increase distressed sales. Ask your agent to give you an accounting of what you can expect in your area. These stats will give you an overall view of market activity and where challenges are likely to surface. Ask your agent to explain each and how it will affect your ability to sell your home.

Some agents provide **graphs** – I'm not crazy about them as I find all those squiggly lines difficult to follow, and a software program – which the agent may or may not understand, usually cranks them out. Ask for percentages – their clarity is helpful.

Financial Climate
In other words, how hard is it to get a loan closed in your area?

This varies widely. "Dodd Frank" legislation became reality in January 2014 – strengthens qualifying requirements for homebuyers. Most are confused as to exactly what the law will mean – time will tell. Additionally, lowered down payments (to 3%), and other inducements are aimed at getting the first time (Millennial) buyer into the housing market. The three underwriting basics: debt to income ratios, loan to value, and credit scores are still tight. Keep in mind this is an uneven recovery. In some areas of the country, there are bubble fears emerging. In others, there's still a backlog of listing inventory.

The agent can provide a picture of the lending climate very clearly – and since you'll want every possible assurance that the Buyer whose offer you accept and take your house off the market for has a better than average chance of getting their loan closed (approval letters are not a guarantee), these stats matter. The professional agent will explain how they work to insure that your buyer has solid financing – do not expect guarantees. Their knowledge of area lending professionals that have high rates of closed loans will be a part of the service they provide. Expect two recommendations for a mortgage professional.

Look for **lending information** that address these issues:

Interest rates, discount points and an overview of fees charged along with the pros/cons of various loan programs.

% Of loans that have appraisal issues
% Of loans that fall-thru
% Of loan applications that actually close.
% Of loans that close on time

Amount of loan volume they have closed in the past 12 months.

Agent's Performance Results
What constitutes skill today? Bottom line, skill is the ability of the agent to get consistent results for their clients in a timely manner. A professional agent will provide you with their

professional stats that showcase their ability to get results for their clients in the current market. It is useful and necessary for the seller to have a reference point for comparison using the agent's statistics. This comparison is two-fold.

First, using the *market average* for all agents, which can be determined comparing the information to the MLS average for all agents.

Second, a comparison should be made *between each agent* who is competing to list your home.

These stats tell the most important part of the story in an objective manner.

Ethics. Ask the prospective agent if they have had or have any complaints/litigations naming them – sadly the industry does a poor job of policing itself. I also happen to believe that it is unethical for an agent to over-price a listing and represent that they will do the job required – and the numbers don't back this claim up. In the industry, we call this "buying a listing" – it's tempting but in the end, it will cost you money. Historically, the longer the time a property sits on the market, the lower the eventual sales price – buyers view it as 'distressed' and expect a deal from the Seller.

Questions to be asked and answered:

Days on the Market – this represents the average time on the market for the agent's listing inventory. This number can and will cost you money. Think of it this way: what will a longer time on market cost you in number of mortgage payments and upkeep and the eventual lowering of the sales price. Also important to note that usually the first question posed by buyers is, "How long has the property been on the market"? *I am aware that at this writing (early 2015), some markets have little inventory and buyers are engaging in 'bidding wars'. Even in these markets, there is inventory that is overpriced that sits unsold. In the minds of today's buyer, there is a difference in you overpricing a property and the price being driven up by buyers in a bidding war.*

ASK: What is your average Days On Market for your listing inventory in the last 12 months as compared to the MLS and/or as compared to the agents they are competing against for your listing. Stress that the number you are looking for is DOM computed from the original listing date until under contract.

Percentage of Listings Sold – The agent's primary job is to sell the listings they take – that's the job they are hired to do. Some agents like to tout their large number of listings – the more important number is the percentage that they have actually sold and closed.

ASK: How many listings have you (the agent) taken in the last twelve months? What percentage of your listings taken in the past 12months have you sold?

Actual Sales Price vs. *Original* List Price – If they can't price well it's highly unlikely you'll get your property sold today. An agent's ability to price correctly is the valued skill in current market conditions. It is your guide as to whether the advice you are getting is credible. *Some agents are avoiding this scrutiny by making the pricing comparison between Actual Sales Price vs. Last List Price – not Original List Price. Make sure that distinction is made to **Original** List Price.* Doing so obscures the price reductions taken and lessens the actual time on market.

ASK: What is the percentage of difference between the actual sales price and **original** list price for the listings that you listed and that have sold in the last twelve months?

Agents may go on about being Top Producers; having Market Share etc. Put your emphasis on those stats that I listed here – they reflect the agent's ability to get results for you under current market conditions. They tell a truer story of their ability.

I've had many agents comment to me that they just couldn't deliver the correct pricing message – fearing that the Sellers wouldn't "like" them. I wonder how much the agent was liked when their failure to do their job cost their client thousands of dollars due to longer time on the market?

On the flip side, Sellers often fall for the promise of the highest price – make sure the stats can back up the agent's claim – many agents 'buy' listings by promising prices they can't deliver – and in the long run, this will cost you money as inevitably you go through price reductions and time on the market to attract today's buyer.

Even if you could find a buyer willing to overpay, it's unlikely that the property will appraise. If the buyer makes representations that they will pay the appraisal difference – your agent must verify that the buyer has the financial ability to deliver.

Agency – or how you will be represented in the sale

Agency/representation **varies by state** – and you are entitled to know what these laws mean in your state. They can vary, as agency, transactional broker, designated agent etc. – make sure you understand your options in your state.

Expect the presenting agent to give you an overview of these laws and how they can affect your interests in the transaction. Have a clear picture of what your agent can and cannot do on your behalf.

Dual Agency
Dual Agency exists when your listing agent also sells the house to a buyer - who is not represented by another agent. This is not in your best interests. No matter how skilled the agent – difficult to represent both sides to the transaction effectively. Explore your options here and be sure you are represented fairly.

Dual agency can also be created when two separate agents both work with the same company – one representing the Seller and one represents the Buyer. In some states, it is then that the *company* becomes the Dual Agent and each agent then represents their client. A professional will explain and offer assurances as to how the confidentiality for each client is handled within the firm.

Agency and representation agreements are put in writing and signed off on by all parties.

Too many times I have witnessed agents forget who they are representing and work to get the deal closed instead – make sure that you agree to all terms as contract provisions get negotiated.

Careful of Dual Agency – I favor each party to the transaction having representation.

Marketing Proposal
After learning about:

Your market conditions and how they can affect the sale of your home;

Finance/liquidity issues in your area;

The agent's performance data;

Your options for representation – what the agent can and cannot do on your behalf in the transaction based on state law;

A professional presentation will next address how your property will be marketed.

Here look for *points of differentiation* between agents/companies.

Most marketing is done online today and is mobile – print ads accounted for less than 1%

of transactions in 2012 according to National Association of Realtors – people want complete and up to date information – and buyers do a lot of research online before contacting an agent and viewing property.

If an agent touts print ads – have them show you the stats for their results – this is passive marketing and doesn't offer much value today. Advertising Open Houses can be the exception – as they are happening the same day as the ad. I prefer print ads referring potential buyers to a website which lists all Open Houses with complete information and directions.

Online Marketing: Websites and Lead Follow-up

Websites and online presence are not created equal. Check out company/agent websites before your appointment, if possible. Look at their listing inventory displays – check for consistency – do all company listings have videos? If listings lack this, it shows that there is no company standard or policy and your listing may meet the same fate. Buyers rarely bother with properties without visuals and full information. Is the website mobile (which means it can be accessed by mobile devices)? Mobile access to online information is critical.

As you peruse their website, look for things that would bring a consumer in – information about neighborhoods and communities and 'walkable' profiles. Note the links with school information; mortgage information; rentals; area health care; recreational amenities and maps. These are pretty basic and help to keep a consumer coming back to the site – important to note that real estate websites offer full access to every listing in their MLS – some push their listings first – I like full and easy access to all. Give the consumer what the consumer wants and they return. No signups, just full access to information and make it mobile.

An agent fluent in the value of online marketing will provide this information for their website:

Total visits: average/day; unique visitors; new visitors
Total page views: average page views/day
Average Pages/Visit
Average Time on Site – increasingly important
Average Bounce Rate

These stats *compared to industry averages* in those areas will give you a clearer picture of their traffic and whether consumers are finding what they want from them online.

Online Lead Response

Next in importance to a fully functioning website is **timely lead response**. This is important to you. The agent can give you an overview of the company's policy and procedure on this. All of this may seem like a lot – considering the online emphasis, doesn't it make sense? Also, you'll want assurances of timely **follow up** of online leads – best way to discover this is to go on the site and ask to be contacted about a listing. Response time is best within one minute and should be no longer than five minutes.

Most online consumers will do research and the timeline from contact and purchase is decreasing each year. The agent can explain how these inquiries are handled.

The latest National Association of Realtors research for the online time line reports 40% of online buyers 4 months away from a decision and 24% of online lookers ready to buy or sell that same day. This is an amazing shift to a shorter time line and you'll want to be assured that these leads are handled effectively.

The WAV Group (Real Estate Research and consulting group) evaluated agent responsiveness in in December

2013 by becoming a homebuyer lead across hundreds of brokerages in 11 states. Their findings may shock you:

- *48% of buyer inquiries were NEVER responded to.*
- *Average number of call back attempts after the initial contact was 1.5*
- *Average number of email contact attempts was 2.07*
- *Average response time was 917 minutes (15.29 hours).*

Other points of marketing differentiation:
If company stats are a concern, I have listed some that may give you insight in to company training standards and policy and procedure.

Company stats – for the same categories as the agent – and as well as:
Per person production,
Online lead conversion rate,
Training offerings and requirements and
A minimum production standard.

These speak to more highly skilled sales force and standards within the company.

Most of the other things you'll learn about will be examples of "red sign, blue sign, yellow sign" – not much difference in companies. **The agent's ability to secure results for their client matter most.**

Pricing Proposal

The **absorption rate pricing analysis** is the most up to date and effective way to price effectively today. Absorption Rate Analysis Pricing is inventory based approach and gives you a clearer picture of your total competition in your market. CMA's use limited data and don't provide a complete picture of your competition. Your 'currently for sale' competition matters most in pricing your property because that's what the buyer is comparing you against.

You are trying to attract today's buyer – scared, skeptical and mistrustful in this economy– and so you have to have an insight to what's important to them. What's most important to them? The 'deal' – **they fear overpaying** – and so look in more expanded areas for the 'right' house. *Won't you have a similar mindset and priorities when you purchase your next property?* Next to price, condition and location matter. Make no mistake price conquers obstacles.

We have been living through a collapse in the housing industry – don't underestimate the effect it has had – not only on the market but also on the consumer. You'd have to have been living on Mars the past several years to think that buyers have forgotten the experiences of the 'great recession' – and no, your house is not special enough to get a buyer to overpay or an appraiser to appraise it.

Even if you could find such a buyer – finding a lender may be another story – lenders are not into risk these days. "Dodd –Frank" legislation is sure to have an impact as well (Jan 2014).

In the Absorption Rate Analysis formula (form follows), you will notice an "**adjusted sales total**". This is used when there are high numbers of "fall thru" (contracts ratified that do not close) and the sales total has to be adjusted to give the clear picture. If this is necessary in your market, expect your agent to explain it.

Some markets were not as hard hit or have bounced back more strongly than the average – the numbers will bear this out, if you're lucky enough to be located in one.

Also, some areas did not experience huge price 'run-ups' and still have steady employment – these areas will exhibit more stable data.

Let the numbers be your guide – they don't lie.

A good agent will explain the absorption rate analysis and also **re evaluate it every 30 days**. Markets move and change and you'll need to move with it. Pricing is the important opportunity today.

Important that the data pulled for the analysis reflect *recent* sales activity – going back just two months – think of your market conditions today (improving in most areas) as opposed to a year ago – big changes! A more current analysis provides the best guide for accuracy.

Absorption Rate Analysis on Contingent Offers

In some markets, offers to purchase come with contingencies attached – e.g., the offer to purchase is contingent based on the sale of the buyer's current home. If you should get such an offer, a professional agent will protect your interests by doing an absorption rate pricing analysis on the buyer's current home to see if it's competitively priced to sell (not all agents use absorption rate analysis to price) and offer more thorough advice as to whether or not to accept the contingent offer.

I had clients in North Carolina who received an offer on one of their listings that included a contingency on the sale of a home in another state (where I happen to live). The client called for my advice and I told them to counter only after an absorption rate analysis had been done on the out of state property. The out-of-state agent was irate – she didn't use this pricing analysis and had been in real estate 30 years. The analysis resulted in a price reduction of nearly 30 thousand dollars – and resulted in a sale within three weeks. The buyer was then able to purchase the house in North Carolina. The seller's interests were protected.

I've included the "Absorption Rate Analysis Report' form so that you'll know what to look for – make sure the agent clearly explains the data. Graphs are difficult to follow and remember the agent did not compile the graph – a software program did it for them.

nGardner Group

Absorption Rate Analysis Report

Date of report

Property Address

Geographic areas studied for this analysis:

1.

2.

3.

4.

Price range studied for this analysis: _____ - _____

Total number active listings studied _____

Number of listings pending (UC) _____ + number of listings closed _____ =

total sold listings _____. Subtract % of fall-thru and explain **adjusted** sales total _____.

Divide total active listings _____ by number of average sales per month _____

= _____ months of inventory in price range and geographic areas studied.

In today's market, you must be priced below the competition in order to draw the attention of today's buyer.

www.ngardnergroup.com

Back-up Mortgage Approval

The listing agent can also cover the need for 'Back-up Mortgage Approval". This may be needed today because of tight lending requirements and if there is a high rate of loan denials in your market.

Professional agents know which lenders are making and closing loans in their markets and which are not. Back-up mortgage approval better insures (not guarantees) that a buyer can close on their loan and the sale of your home.

Some agents have voiced objections to asking for back-up mortgage approval, fearing buyer or buyer agent objections and possible loss of the sale. If that's a concern, have the lender representing the buyer provide the **'liquidity stats**" listed in this book to give you more assurance of their ability to close the loan.

An agent with a company I had trained on this the previous year, told me about a sale that fell-thru – her listing @ $800,000 because the buyer's lender couldn't deliver. She was visibly upset. I asked her if she required back-up mortgage approval when the offer was presented. She said that she had not. I then asked her how her seller client would respond if they knew that she had been trained to do so – but had not. She was silent. In my opinion, she failed to represent her Seller client and do her job.

Note: Your contract is not fully ratified until all contingencies are removed.

Communication During the Listing Period

Expect agent follow-up a **minimum of once weekly**. The listing agent should cover all marketing efforts and showing feedback from property showings (if available). Written accountings are helpful and can be emailed to you in advance. Be sure to let your agent know how you wish to communicate – phone, email, text messages – whatever works best for **you**.

The Absorption Rate Analysis should be re evaluated every 30 days. Pricing is adjusted accordingly. Markets are volatile and there is a lot that can and does affect them – your property must be priced with this in mind.

Offer of Additional Services

Agents can also provide a list of outside vendors that can help you with maintenance issues. Home repair, cleaning services, and moving etc. – the agent can provide you with a list of recommendations (though not guaranteed) and all should be licensed and bonded for your protection.

The Listing Agreement
Most of these are boilerplate documents and they represent ALL that Sellers can hold an agent or a company accountable to performing.

Look for an agent and company that offer a **guarantee of service** – stating clearly all that has been promised during the presentation – attached as part of the listing agreement. This guarantee also gives the Seller the right to terminate the listing if they are unhappy with the performance of the agent as promised in the agreement.

Another consideration here is the **term of the agreement** – if an agent knows what they are doing and has advised you accordingly – ninety (90) days should be maximum time necessary to sell your property – and I am being generous here.

CONFLICTS OF INTEREST
In addition to Dual Agency (referenced earlier) there are other possible conflicts to be aware of:

Pre-marketing the listing aka "Coming Soon"
Careful of agents who want to **pre-market the listing** themselves or within the company for

an initial period - these may be common real estate practices that can benefit the agent or the company but not their clients. **It is in the best interest of the Seller for their property to be marketed to as many people as possible from the onset – to help insure best possible offer.** Hire an agent who put clients first.

If an agent feels this is a benefit to you (given current market conditions), make sure that a specific time line is set to present all offers. For example, in a strong market with little inventory, offers can be held for a number of days to ensure that the Seller has access to all of them before deciding which offer to accept.

Zillow.com has offered a 30-day pre list designation on listings for agents who advertise with them. Again, this can benefit the agent and not you.

Agent Compensation
Commissions are negotiable. Most listing companies charge between 5-6% of the final sales price. That amount is then split (usually) 50/50 with the selling company.

You'll need to know what amount you are being charged (at close of sale) and how the commission is split between listing and selling company and offered in the MLS. Some agents/companies do not split the commission with the selling company 50/50 – make sure you are clear on their practice and the reasoning behind it.

In-House Commission Bonus
It is still common practice today to offer in-house bonuses. This means there is an incentive to the selling (buyers) agent if they are affiliated with the same company as your listing (sellers) agent. In any event, all compensation should be disclosed and agreed in writing.

This could also mean *Dual Agency* (agents representing both client/sides of the transaction work for the same company) – if you agree, your agent should provide information on confidentiality practices within the company.

I like a level playing field. The compensation is only that which is offered in the MLS and fully disclosed to the client.

Seller Net Sheet
This is an accounting of your projected proceeds from the sale and used to be required in some states. It's making a comeback.

Ask for one – the professional agent will prepare and offer it to you. First, when the house is listed and it is based on a *projected* sales price. Finally, at the time of contract ratification – based on the actual sales price of the property. If you have disclosed all liens etc., it should be a close match to your proceeds at close of sale. Adjustments may be made to it based on any late monetary concessions by either party (e.g., home inspection; pest inspection adjustments).

Administrative Details of the Transaction

In addition, expect the agent to cover the following:

Listing Agreement – this is the legally binding document that creates the contract between the seller and the listing company and agent. Note – this agreement outlines what is legally enforceable. You want to have any 'service guarantees' attached to and made apart of this agreement. Doing so makes them enforceable. In other words, if an agent fails to do what has been promised and you are not satisfied, you can terminate the contract and hire someone else.

Home Inspection – expect the Buyer to want one – it's in their best interest. Some sellers are having an inspection completed **before** listing the property – and complete needed repairs beforehand – and then make the information available to buyers. Understand that once you know you have a problem with the property you are obliged to fix it or disclose it. The buyers may opt for their own home inspection anyway; remember there is a trust issue out there.

Important to note, that when you are dealing with home inspection issues, you are **renegotiating your contract**. Contracts can "fall-thru" at this point – your agent can provide information on how much of this (% of transactions) is occurring in your market. Just understand what's at risk here as you renegotiate terms.

Pest Inspection – lender requirement.

Environmental and other disclosures – these vary by state. Expect the agent to explain.

Home Warranty – most cover the property while it's on the market (not all things are covered during the listing period) and transfer to the buyer at settlement. I've always believed that warranties were in everyone's best interests. The cost is minimal and not paid until settlement/closing of escrow.

HOA or POA Docs – if your property is located in a neighborhood with a "Home Owners Association" it is common and required practice that documents be released within a certain time frame – the listing agent requests this to fulfill the contract and must make sure the documents are delivered to the buyer in a timely manner.

Transaction Management – get an explanation of who will be doing what – and how you can contact them – and how and when you will be contacted with updates.

Many companies have transaction coordinators whose job it is to take care of the administrative aspects of the sale – usually from contract to closing. Some real estate and mortgage companies have online access to the information for your convenience.

The time period between *under contract and the closing of the sale* can be stressful for you. Know what's going on – expect that you will hear from your listing agent at least weekly for updates.

Ask your agent for a checklist of things that must be completed by close of sale. This will help you stay on track and feel more in control. It's normal to feel unglued when faced with moving.

I have provided a '**Seller's Checklist**' to help you stay on track and cover the information that will matter most to **you** during the listing process and sale of your home.

Ask questions and expect answers. It matters.

Good luck with the sale of your property – and if you're going to buy after your sell – then keep reading!

Seller's Checklist

o Pre-Appointment Questions
o Appointment to Preview
   Preview and offer needed repair/maintenance service vendors, if appropriate
o Listing Appointment/Presentation
o Overview of Current Market/Finance Conditions using stats
o Explain client representation
o Marketing Proposal - points of differentiation and positioning with implementation calendar
o DEMONSTRATE I-Lead Capture/Management System
o Pricing – CMA vs. Absorption Rate Analysis – RE EVALUATE @ 30 DAYS
o Absorption rate analysis on all contingent offers
o Backup Mortgage Approval
o Lay out format for future price reductions
o Offer service vendors if not done previously
o Offer Home Warranty
o Documents/ Disclosures
o Listing Agreement and Guarantee of Service
o Compensation and the Seller Net Sheet
o Showing Instructions /Lockbox/Signage
o Administrative details- online transaction management
o Seller Packet
o Seller Follow-up/Follow-thru
o Negotiation of Offer. Use absorption rate analysis to evaluate any contingent offer.
o Home Inspection Renegotiation
o Transaction Management - Contract to Closing Guide
   Weekly communication – the process from contract to closing.
   Offer of additional services:
   Home maintenance; Home Cleaning Services; Moving Company, etc.

BUYER'S GUIDE TO HIRING AN AGENT

PART TWO

IT'S THE LARGEST SINGLE INVESTMENT YOU'RE LIKELY TO MAKE

I find it indefensible that most companies and agents do not offer or train a Buyer Presentation – much in the same way a Seller expects a Listing Presentation – time spent up front explaining the buying process, market conditions, liquidity issues, etc. As a buyer today, it is in your best interest to work with an agent who provides this for you – you'll be better informed and more confident in your decision to purchase.

A professional real estate agent will provide you with advice and counsel based on their knowledge of the market and transaction experience. They will support this data with statistics and analysis to help buyers make better purchase decisions.

The "Buyer 's Checklist" that follows this section provides a list of what you can expect in a buyer presentation.

To be fair, many buyers just want to 'look at houses' in the hopes that they might find something – I think this stems from agents who historically have not taken control (in the way any professional would). Also, many Buyers believe (wrongly) that there's no difference in agents and they do not want to get stuck with an agent they don't like. There are differences. I encourage you to search and find the right agent – this is the largest single investment you're likely to make – hiring the right agent can save you money.

The following is an overview of information you'll need to make your best purchase decision. A skilled professional will take you through this information to make the buying process much easier to navigate. It also enables the agent to do a better job for you – the job you are hiring them to do.

How will you go about finding the right agent to represent you in the purchase?
There are a number of ways this is accomplished. The most utilized way is by referral from your network of family, friends, and colleagues. However you find the agents you will interview – the responsibility lies with you to hire someone who will do an outstanding job for you. Remember, the person who made the referral may not have had this information before they purchased – you do. Do your research now and you'll be the beneficiary.

Referral

Most people choose someone through *referral* – an agent you know or have used before – so you can start there – just be prepared that it might not end there. Friendship is not a necessary requirement – the point is to hire someone who serves your interests and can get the job done. Let **objective** criteria guide you first.

Top Producers

You might assume that hiring a 'top agent' is the way to go. "It ain't necessarily so." Focus on actual results at whatever level the agent produces. Volume is not a sure sign of service (as you define it) – there are other considerations that may be important to you as well. E.g.' you may want/need a lot of hand-holding and frequent communication or you may want to skip the details and get on with finding the right house – either is fine. Just be sure your agent is a good match for your preferences AND can get the job done. The selection of an agent is both objective and subjective.

Buyer's Agents

Some agents only work with Buyers. This is no guarantee of skill or service. Look for the same results and criteria outlined in this section for guidance.

New Agents

Is it a bad idea to hire someone with little or no experience? Again, look for results. In many cases, new agents are better trained than their more experienced counterparts. The new agent will provide you with company results stats, which can give you an indication of their abilities. Listen for their ability to explain and educate you. Also, expect for an accounting of the company-training program they have completed and the amount of oversight that will be provided them (and you) during the transaction.

Agent Teams

Teams usually have agents who specialize in working with Buyers. Again, the numbers will tell you story you need to hear. So ask the questions and pay attention to their answers.

Online Agent Rankings

Objective information about agents is showing up online. There are multiple sites for reviews of real estate agents by former clients – the difficulty arises from the fact that the reviews are subjective and beauty is in the eye of the beholder. What one client values; another may not. Questions also arise about the source of the reviews. Did the reviewer actually work with the agent or did the review come from a relative?

MLS' across the country have different standards for measuring data – most of which favors the real estate community. Some MLS' don't report the "selling side" data and give all focus on the "listing side" of the transaction. A professional will be prepared for this if it exists in their market and will give you an accounting of their results for both sides of the transactions.

Additional Agent Review Sites

You may locate helpful real estate agent profiles and reviews on the following:

Zillow.com

Trulia.com

Redfin.com (not in all markets)

Realtor.com (coming soon)

Yahoo.com

Yelp.com

Google+Local

Facebook

Realsatisfied.com

Stik.com

Zufog.com

Reach150.com

RealEstateRatingz.com

HomeThinking.com

IncredibleAgents.com

RateMyAgent.com

NeighborCity.com

TopAgentsRanked.com

Angie's List
Yahoo Local
CitySearch.com
InsiderPages.com
LinkedIn.com
Har.com (Houston TX market)

Most online agent reviews are subjective – and while, helpful, you want objective information concerning an agent's results. When online reviews turn into online rankings based on an agent's results, they'll be much more useful to you.

If you're checking an agent out on social media sites – recommendations will vary – and you'll have a tough time figuring out the source – which could be a fellow agent, their broker or their grandmother. In short, it's hard to get the info you need in order to make your hiring decision with confidence.

Some real estate professionals have gotten out in front of the issues of results and transparency. These agents have put a link in their email signature that gives an accounting of their results. Agents mat also have added their results data into their agent profiles and onto their websites/pages. Careful here, some misrepresent themselves – verify when you can by checking the history of listed properties.

What you can expect from a qualified professional

Expect an introduction with:
Pre appointment questions on your first contact for preparation purposes;
A first appointment to provide you with an education of market and financial conditions for your area and how they may affect your ability to purchase;
An interview to determine your needs and wants;
Offer of representation; Enforceable Service Guarantees;
Pricing analysis on any property before any offer to purchase is made;
Qualified vendor referrals

to be covered during your first appointment. This takes a little more time than just running out and looking at property – and you'll save big in the long run.

BUYER PRESENTATION
Agent Introduction
If you already know the agent you want to hire – that's fine – as long as they are skilled at doing the job you want them to do. Friends don't always make the best choices – nor do family members – they can cost you a lot –

expect the same from them as you would any professional. This is a business decision about the largest single financial investment you're likely to make.

An agent who has been referred to you will most likely contact you by phone, introduce him or herself to you and ask, "How can I help you?" You will then be able to give them an overview of your situation and set an appointment to meet for the *interview.*

Pre-Appointment Questions
During the first introduction, the agent will ask you a few questions concerning pertinent information that you may not have covered in your introduction so that they can better prepare for their meeting with you. Tell them the truth about your situation – it will all come out anyway – and you'll have fewer hurdles along the way. Honesty is a two way street.

Financing
The professional agent will inquire as to whether you have looked into how/if you will finance your purchase – and will have two lenders contact you to get this part of the process started. Today, most loan applications are made online.

Good questions for a prospective lender and the agent who recommends the lender are:

"What percentage of the loan applications made with you actually close?

How many of your loans have appraisal problems?

How many of the loans close with the same loan terms initially quoted? (Some lenders still reel you in with promises of rates or programs and then switch you into something else, claiming you don't qualify).

How much loan volume have you closed in the last twelve months?

Also, take a look at loan origination fees and other charges you will have to pay. Consider interests rates as well as fees when choosing your lender. As I said earlier, smart agents know who the good lenders are – if you end up getting a list of lenders, this is not a service to you – smart agents know who to recommend to you and understand that this is a valuable service to you as a Buyer.

Also look for a lender that allows for your loan package to be "walked" to another lender if the need arises – you have paid for credit reports and an appraisal etc., and the ability to move that information if the first lender can't deliver can be important to you and will save you money and time.

Again, tell your lender the truth and disclose your financial situation accurately – you owe the truth to the professionals working for you and they will find out anyway.

If you have already started working on your financing – a skilled agent will offer **backup mortgage approval** – liquidity is still tight in some markets – and you'll want the security of knowing you have options should you need them. Also, some lenders don't deliver what they promise and you may want another option.

Buyer Presentation Overview
Initial Appointment – Market, Financial and Absorption Rate Pricing counsel. Agent's Professional Performance Data. Buyer Interview. Offer of Representation. Mode of Communication. Administrative Overview.

Current Market Conditions
First, expect the agent to educate you on *current market conditions* – using supporting data – and how these conditions can affect your ability to buy.

The stats that will matter most to you as a buyer are:

Current Listing Inventory – as compared to previous year

Days on Market – average amount of time a property on market before contract

Current Pendings – as compared to previous year

Closed Transactions – as compared to previous year

Average Sales Price – as compared to previous year

Financial Overview

If this was not covered in your initial conversation, the agent must cover this information now. Finding the right house for you and being able to close on the loan are two different things. You'll want to understand the hurdles that may exist in your market/price range. Refer to *Financing* in the section on "Pre Appointment Questions". Is there anything worse than attaching yourself to a house you can't afford? Go in to this with your eyes wide open.

Also, "Dodd Frank" legislation which debuted in January, 2014 will require 'front and back ratio' compliance – which is a way of saying that it may be tougher for you to qualify for a loan – a good lender will make sure there are no surprises – provided you provide them an accurate accounting of your finances.

In 2015, rates have dropped, down payments reduced and there are other inducements aimed at the first time (Millennial) buyer. The three underwriting basics – loan to value ration, debt to income ratio and credit scores are still tight.

Agent's Professional Results Data

What constitutes skill today? Bottom line, skill is the ability of the agent to get consistent results for their clients in a timely manner. A professional agent will provide you with their **professional stats** that showcase their ability to get results for their clients in the current market. It is useful and necessary for you to have a reference point for comparison using the agent's statistics. This comparison is two-fold.

First, the agent provides the *market average* for all agents, which can be determined averaging the information in the MLS average for all agents and then a comparison is made to the agent's own results.

Second, a comparison should be made *between each agent* who is competing for your business.

These stats tell the most important part of the story in an **objective** manner. Other factors that you may weigh are **subjective** and will vary in importance to the individual.

Ethics

Ask the prospective agent if they have had or have any complaints/litigations naming them – sadly the industry does a poor job of policing itself. I also happen to believe that it is unethical for an agent to over price a listing and represent that they will do the job required – and the numbers don't back this claim up. In the industry, we call this "buying a listing" – it's tempting, but in the end, it will cost you money. Historically, the longer the time a property sits on the market, the lower the eventual sales price – buyers view it as 'distressed' and expect a deal from the Seller.

Absorption Rate Pricing Analysis

As part of the reason you will choose an agent to work with, you should expect guidance on pricing. The Absorption Rate Pricing Analysis approach provides the comprehensive data necessary today. This is a critical reason for choosing an agent to represent you in the transaction. During the initial appointment, the agent will explain how pricing counsel will be given to you when the time comes to make an offer to purchase.

Nancy G Gardner

The Absorption Rate Pricing Analysis is a more comprehensive inventory approach to pricing. It takes into consideration the months of available inventory and the rate at which the inventory is selling to create a clearer picture of market conditions for the property. The outdated CMA is a narrow approach that compares the property to 3-5 similar properties and doesn't give you a picture of the *market f*or that property, considering price point and location and the rate of sale for similar properties.

The analysis will provide you with the information necessary to guide the pricing component of your offer. The skilled agent will take you through this information and do the analysis on any property you are seriously considering.

Absorption Rate Pricing Analysis form follows for your reference

nGardner Group

Absorption Rate Analysis Report

Date of report

Property Address

Geographic areas studied for this analysis:

1.

2.

3.

4.

Price range studied for this analysis: _____ - _____

Total number active listings studied _____

Number of listings pending (UC) _____ + number of listings closed _____ =

total sold listings _____. Subtract % of fall-thru and explain **adjusted** sales total _____.

Divide total active listings _____ by number of average sales per month _____

= _____ months of inventory in price range and geographic areas studied.

In today's market, you must be priced below the competition in order to draw the attention of today's buyer.

www.ngardnergroup.com

Buyer Needs Analysis (Interview)
This is the interview questioning conducted by the agent to determine what you want and need in your new home. Oft times it will help you in nailing down your priorities. It is a necessary part of the picture in order for the agent to preview/select properties that fit your priorities – saving you time in the process.

How will you be represented in the purchase of your home?
I recommend that once you find the right agent that you will work with - that you accept their offer to represent you in the transaction. Buyer Representation or Agency as it is sometimes called – **laws vary by state and your agent will cover your options in your state** - specifies how you can be represented in the purchase. It will also explain the duties of the agent on your behalf. (In some states, there is transactional agency, designated representation etc. – make sure your agent explains). Have a clear understanding of what an agent can and cannot do in the transaction.

If you choose to be represented by an agent, you'll be asked to sign an agreement defining that representation. Initially, you may want to limit the time frame and or the scope of the area for the agreement – you can extend it if you want.

Service Guarantees

Unless you have a signed agreement of representation (as allowed by your state), you don't have much to support you other than general legal directives. The smart agent provides 'service guarantees' for what you can expect working with them and makes them part of the representation agreement. The guarantee lays out what they will do for you and allows you to terminate if they do not deliver.

Conflicts of Interest

Most of these stem from **Dual Agency** – which is generally *not* in your best interests to allow in the transaction. Dual agency occurs when a single agent represents both parties (buyer and seller) to the transaction. Dual Agency can also arise when both agents involved in a transaction work for the same company. In this case, expect your agent to fully explain company policy and procedure on confidentiality. Make sure that you are clear as to what the agent you work with can and cannot do based on how you are represented in the purchase. And if the agent can't clearly explain their role, how can you expect them to execute clearly on your behalf? Explore your options here.

Viewing Properties

As much information as there is online, unless you already know the area and the considered property – view in broad daylight. If you are interested, take your time. Go back through the house again.

If you do not know the area, the agent will show you areas and neighborhoods first so that you have a better feel for your commute, local amenities, school locations and any special interests you may have.

New Homes

If you are considering the purchase of a new home, you will most likely be using the builder's contract and for the most part agreeing to their terms. In a 'hot market' there is little or no room for negotiation. Be sure to read the contract – I have seen ones that automatically void if a buyer walks on to the property while it's under construction. Builders may be more amenable after the housing collapse – just be informed. When it comes to price, most negotiation occurs in the pricing of 'options', keeping the listed price for the property intact. Also, be sure to question the builder's reputation – they are not all created equal.

Re-evaluation
It sometimes happens that after viewing several properties, your priorities will change. Oft times this occurs when a buyer realizes that what they can afford does not have the purchasing power they had imagined.

A professional agent should ask you – after viewing 6-8 properties – and you've seen nothing that you are interested in – to re evaluate your priorities to learn what has changed for you and how they can do a better job of finding properties that better suit your needs/wants. This is all a part of the process – don't be reluctant to communicate this to your agent.

Writing/Making an Offer to Purchase
The professional agent will first contact the listing agent to learn of any additional information that could affect you and your offer. Failure to do so can also result in you losing out because another offer was being negotiated without the knowledge that your offer was in the works.

The professional agent will do an "Absorption Rate Pricing Analysis" to aid in positioning your offer in relation to price. This analysis will accompany your offer and should be explained to the seller by the buyer's (your) agent. The buyer cannot count on the seller's agent being able to explain the pricing analysis competently and in a way that looks out for your best interests.

In some markets, agents for the buyer are not given access to the seller to present the offer. This is an outdated practice and it assumes that the listing agent can do the best job of presenting your offer. All your agent can do is make the request to present your offer in person – much of the time it's left to the listing agent.

Contingencies

There are other aspects of your offer that matter: *Appraisal terms; Home Inspection terms; Pest Inspection terms; Conveyances; HOA/POA documents and inquiry; Date of Closing the Sale.* The professional will discuss each with you and explain their possible impact on your offer being accepted and they will represent your (buyer's) interest in each.

Keep in mind that if you have communicated to your agent that a particular property is important to you – the advice you get may reflect that – *and* be accompanied with the necessary counsel of any risk you may be incurring accordingly. *E.g., if you as buyer on a property decide to forego the appraisal clause in the contract (which basically says that the property must appraise to get the financing), you will be responsible for making up the difference ($$$$).* As of this writing, appraisals can be a barrier in securing financing – there are still a lot of lenders who do not want to make loans without a *lot* of assurance. There were a lot of loans that should have never been made during the real estate bubble – and there are a lot of loans being denied now that shouldn't be – it can be tough out there!

Home Inspection – by all means, have a home inspection. They teach you a lot about the property you are buying including an estimate of the life and functions of many of the main systems of the property. A professional agent will refer you to two home inspectors who are known to do a thorough job. The agent can also advise you on the percentage of contracts that fall-thru in your market as a result of failed inspection negotiations. It's a point worth making that any time you renegotiate elements within the contract that it can result in the contract falling apart.

It's worth noting that in strong markets, buyers may forego the home inspection due to fear of losing the home in a bidding war.

HOA/POA documents and an in-depth inquiry – these documents are required in most states and must be delivered to the buyer within a certain time frame. The professional agent may also request an *in depth inquiry* to better insure that you have all pertinent neighborhood information regarding special assessments, up coming expenditures, etc. In areas where there have been multiple foreclosures, many of these associations have maintained these properties and the costs are passed on to the membership. Get the whole story. Be clear on what monies you might be expected to pay beyond dues.

Pest Inspections - the lender will require it – and it's in your best interest. Seller will take care of any issues that arise. If you are a cash buyer – have a pest inspection conducted on your own behalf.

Date of close of sale/escrow – this can be an important negotiating issue based on the needs/motivations of the seller of the property. Most occur at the end of the month. Unless that date is a priority to you – why not close the sale at another time during the month – when vendors are less busy – and have more time to insure that your closing goes smoothly and that deadlines are met?

Presentation of your offer

A real estate professional will also explain that he/she will present your offer themselves to insure that the seller of the property understands how your offer price point was determined. Many agents still do not know how to do the absorption rate pricing analysis and will be at a loss as to how to adequately explain it.

Having your agent present your offer in person is not a regular practice today. Most are faxed and followed with a phone call if necessary. This is a lazy practice and it does not fully represent you.

Ask your agent how your offer to purchase will be presented to the seller. It matters.

Many Seller agents' block this practice – properly done, it is not intrusive. The Buyer's agent meets with both the Seller and their agent and explains the offer, answers any questions and then leaves. The Seller can then discuss the offer with their agent and either accepts, rejects or counters the offer to purchase.

Contract ratification to closing

A professional agent will maintain consistent communication and keep you updated and informed on a regular basis.

Many companies have online transaction management – a site where you will access your paperwork timeline and view the updates.

Some agents have assistants that cover the administrative aspects of the sale – this can be helpful – as they keep regular office hours, as opposed to your agent who may be working 'in the field'.

Either way, a professional communicates consistently and tells you what you can expect – in the manner that you prefer.

Buyer's Net Sheet
This is an accounting of expected costs/monies required at close of sale. Lenders provide this to buyers based on loan types, down payments etc. The final amount can change from the original estimate due to changes in terms and/ or concessions made during renegotiation.

Additional Services
A professional agent will provide a list of proven vendors for the buyer, as you need them. House cleaners; moving companies; home repair contractors etc. No agent can be expected to guarantee a vendor, and can recommend based on

prior experience. All should be licensed and bonded for your protection.

Home warranty – some properties offer the buyer a home warranty – for others it can be a negotiable item. It's a good idea – especially if it's important to you not to incur unexpected housing expense – the warranty renews annually. The cost is paid at close of sale/escrow.

Agent Compensation

Who is responsible for compensating your buyer agent? In the majority of markets, compensation is stated as "based on what is offered in the MLS". Commissions are traditionally shared equally between the listing company and the selling company and then split with the agent based on their 'split' with their company. Ask any questions you have about how the agent will be paid UP FRONT.

Conflicts of interest

Dual Agency – as with the Seller, the agent is working on both sides of the transaction – the agent would be selling you a property that they have listed. If this is the case, you can ask to have another agent assigned to represent you – dual agency means that no one in the sale is represented and I do not recommend it. Explore your options here.

Another way Dual Agency occurs is when an agent sells you a house that is listed with another agent in their company. Ask for an explanation of company policy that ensures that your information will be kept confidential.

In-House Commission Bonus

Many real estate companies offer a commission bonus for 'in-house' sales – the sale of a company listing – to incentivize such sales. Some companies even recruit agents with this bonus, explaining that they have a large listing inventory and that the likelihood of an in-house sale will pay them a bonus.

Seller Offer of Bonus

Another **conflict** can arise from the offer of a sales bonus – an amount paid by the seller in addition to the commission.

Confirm with your agent how these will be handled. Full and complete disclosure is to be expected.

Close of sale/escrow

In some states an attorney is required; not so in others. Your agent will cover your options here and recommend professionals.

Make sure you are informed on "taking title" to the property – it varies – and it can matter a lot given that relationships can and do vary widely. This is a legal issue.

You will sign your loan note and related paperwork.

A document called the HUD1 will outline your costs and any additional payments required to meet the terms of the contract.

I've included a "Buyer Checklist" to help you stay on track.

Good luck with your purchase! I hope you love living there and that you will recommend the agent you worked with – because they did a great job for you!

Buyer's Checklist

Via Telephone:
- o   Agent Introduction
- o   Buyer Pre Appointment Questions – for appointment preparation
- o   Begin Loan Approval /Backup – *loan reps to call buyer*
- o   Make initial buyer appointment (*at the office*)
- o   Confirm appointment –directions?

Initial Appointment:
- o   Buyer Presentation Overview – *understand the process and market/ finance conditions (with market stats)*
- o   Agent's Performance Results Data
- o   Absorption pricing counseling to position Offer
- o   Buyer Needs Analysis
- o   Offer Representation Offerings/Options (*Paraphrased for your state*) Service Guarantees.
- o   Final Loan Approval
- o   MLS Search
- o   Offer of representation
- o   Viewing Properties: Neighborhoods v. Property

After Showing Several Properties:
- o   Re-evaluate (*if necessary*). *After viewing 6-8 houses sit down with the agent and discuss whether the agent missed something or that your priorities have changed – don't be shy about giving the agent feedback – it will help them do a better job for you.*

And Finally:
- o   Write Offer using Absorption Rate Pricing analysis
- o   Review contract to closing events. Home Inspection re-negotiation. In depth HOA inquiry.
- o   On line transaction management
- o   Contract to closing guideline
- o   Weekly feedback/follow up
- o   Customer Follow up Call – one month after closing

Offer Additional Services:
- o   Moving Company referral
- o   Cleaning Service referral:
- o   Utilities hookup information and reminder
- o   Home services contractor referrals
- o   Home warranty